The Dutch, the Germans and the Jews

Jan Herman Brinks

The Dutch, the Germans and the Jews

Aspekt Publishers

The Dutch, the Germans and the Jews

© 2016 ASPEKT Publishers
© Jan Herman Brinks

Amersfoortsestraat 27, 3769 AD Soesterberg, Nederland
info@uitgeverijaspekt.nl - http://www.uitgeverijaspekt.nl

Omslagontwerp: Maarten Bakker
Binnenwerk: Thomas Wunderink

ISBN: 9789463380379
NUR: 680

All rights reserved. No part of this book may be reproduced, stored in a retrieval system, or transmitted in any form or by any means, electronic, electrostatic, magnetic tape, mechanical, photocopying, recording or otherwise, without the written permission of the publisher: Uitgeverij Aspekt, Amersfoortseweg 27, 3769 AD Soesterberg, Nederland.

Preface

When I wrote 'The Dutch, the Germans and the Jews' in 1999, I did not realize that the article was to become so controversial. With regard to the wartime record of the Netherlands, the Dutch had, over the years, constructed a national image of heroic resistance against the German occupier. This image was complemented by a stress on Dutch support of its persecuted Jewish citizens. My article noted, however, that little was further from the truth. On virtually all levels, before and even during the war, a substantial number of Dutch people collaborated with Nazi Germany. The Jewish Dutch received only scant support.

The first two decades after the war were, as far as this legacy was concerned, characterized by repression and denial. Leaving the past behind was a survival strategy; expressing normality became something of an ideological programme. The fate of the Dutch Jews was hardly an issue. In truth, though--except for a two-day strike in February 1941--Jews did not receive much solidarity from their non-Jewish compatriots.

This short survey is the outcome of an investigation I undertook when I was a research fellow at Birkbeck College in London. Aside from correcting a few typographical errors, I did not change the original text that was published in *History Today*. The Dutch reactions to my findings, from both private individuals and scholars, were rather hostile. It seemed I had touched a raw nerve. It is safe to argue that even now for Dutch historians, to write a critical history of Dutch collaboration with Nazi Germany is nearly a taboo act; the expressing of such a stance might quickly develop into a career-limiting move.

A good philosopher, according to Nietzsche, has to be the bad conscience of his time. I argue that this duty also applies to historians and journalists. I hope that my critique will be seen as an invitation to researchers to take a closer look at this black page in Dutch history.

Groningen, March 2016.

The Dutch, the Germans and the Jews

Careful readers of the compelling diary of Anne Frank might notice that her hiding place was betrayed to the Nazis by Dutch neighbours, without drawing wider conclusions about the behaviour of Dutch people during the occupation by the Third Reich.

In light of the latest revelations of Dutch complicity in the acquisition of Jewish money, artworks and other treasure by the Nazis, contemporary Dutch historians are engaged in a wholesale revision of the relationship between the Netherlands and the Hitler regime.

This introspection has been overdue for a long time. Contrary to popular belief, a far from harmless rapprochement between the Dutch and Nazi Germany had already taken place during the inter-war period. At the root of this were both economic and ideological motives, i.e. a virulent anti-communism that had penetrated deeply into the Dutch elites. In 1917 the Bolsheviks had annulled all foreign debts. However, in the Netherlands it was not the authorities or banks that had to suffer, but almost exclusively private individuals who had invested heavily in the Tsarist empire. The then astronomical sum of 1 billion guilders was at stake;

more than the sum total of annual Dutch expenditure.[1]

This anti-communism was not free from anti-Semitic undertones. The minister of the Netherlands in Russia, Oudendijk, for example, argued in a report in 1918: 'I consider that the immediate suppression of Bolshevism is the greatest issue now before the world, not even excluding the war (First World War, JHB) which is still raging, and unless as above stated Bolshevism is nipped in the bud immediately it is bound to spread in one form or another over Europe and the whole world as it is organised and worked by Jews who have no nationality, and whose one object is to destroy for their own ends the existing order of things. The only manner in which this danger could be averted would be collective action on the part of all powers.'[2]

The anger among the Dutch elites about financial losses and fear of the Bolsheviks may have contributed to the fact that the Dutch bourgeoisie was initially susceptible to Hitler's anti-Bolshevism, condoning his anti-Semitism for a long time.

After 1935, close Dutch-German collaboration was apparent in the arrest of 'Marxist and Jewish elements'.[3] The immediate cause of this collaboration was the Dutch government's fear of a stream of refugees from the German *Saar*, which had decided by plebiscite, on 13 January 1935, to unite with the German *Reich*. Many left-wing and Jewish Germans who had taken refuge there after Hitler came to power in 1933 now decided to flee.

Fear of 'Judeo-Bolshevism'

On 16 January 1935, three days after the ballot in the *Saar*, the attorney-general of Amsterdam, A. Baron van Harinxma thoe Slooten, argued, at the instigation of the Gestapo, in a confidential letter to the minister of Justice, J.R.H. van Schaik:

> 'In my opinion the establishment of concentration camps where all undesirable communist elements could be sheltered who, in spite of the actions already taken by Your Excellency, will yet enter the Netherlands from the *Saar* and who are highly dangerous, not only with regard to internal peace but also because of less pleasant complications abroad, seems inescapably necessary.'[4]

In March of 1935 the Fortress Honswijk south of Utrecht was fitted up for this purpose.

Among the Dutch authorities, especially among the senior staff of police, there were quite a few who already offered their services to the Nazis during the interwar years. They saw Hitler as the most reliable defence against the 'Red peril'. The police commissioner of Amsterdam, K.H. Broekhoff, for example, personally reported in 1935 to the Gestapo in Berlin that the Dutch Minister of Defence would co-operate in the mutual fight against *'kommunistische und marxistische Umtriebe'* ('Communist and Marxist machinations'). Under the pen-name of 'David' Broekhoff took care of the exchange of information through which 250 Ger-

Mr. P.A.V. baron van Harinxma thoe Slooten

J.H.R.van Schaik

man 'illegals' who had fled to the Netherlands immediately after the occupation in May 1940 were arrested by the Nazi Security Police.[5] Rotterdam's then chief commissioner of police, Mr. L. Einthoven, too, figured, together with 17 other Dutch police officers considered to be *'deutschfreundlich'* (pro-German) in a list of names of the *Gestapo*.[6]

This pro-German atmosphere also affected the Dutch media. According to the Dutch historian Pieter Geyl, who also worked as a journalist for the *Nieuwe Rotterdamse Courant*, this very influential newspaper sacked its Jewish foreign editor and acting editor-in-chief, Marcus van Blankenstein, as early as 1936 because he took too critical and close a look at the developments in Germany.[7] In the opinion of the staff, whose interests were bound up with Rotterdam's port barons, it was better to avoid harming the interests of the state and the economy. So that was why incurring Germany's displeasure had to be avoided.[8]

At the wedding of the future queen, Princess Juliana, to the German-born Bernhard zur Lippe-Biesterfeld in January 1937, it became clear just how closely associated the Dutch elite was with Nazi Germany. Prince Bernhard, who, with his brother, had been a member of the Reiter-SS, the mounted section of the Nazi elite unit – was surrounded by friends who were active National Socialists. During a pre-wedding gala in the Building of the Arts and Sciences in The Hague, the *Horst Wessel Lied*, the Nazi anthem, was sung.

Marriage Juliana and Bernhard

Pieter Geyl

Bernhard van Lippe-Biesterfeld

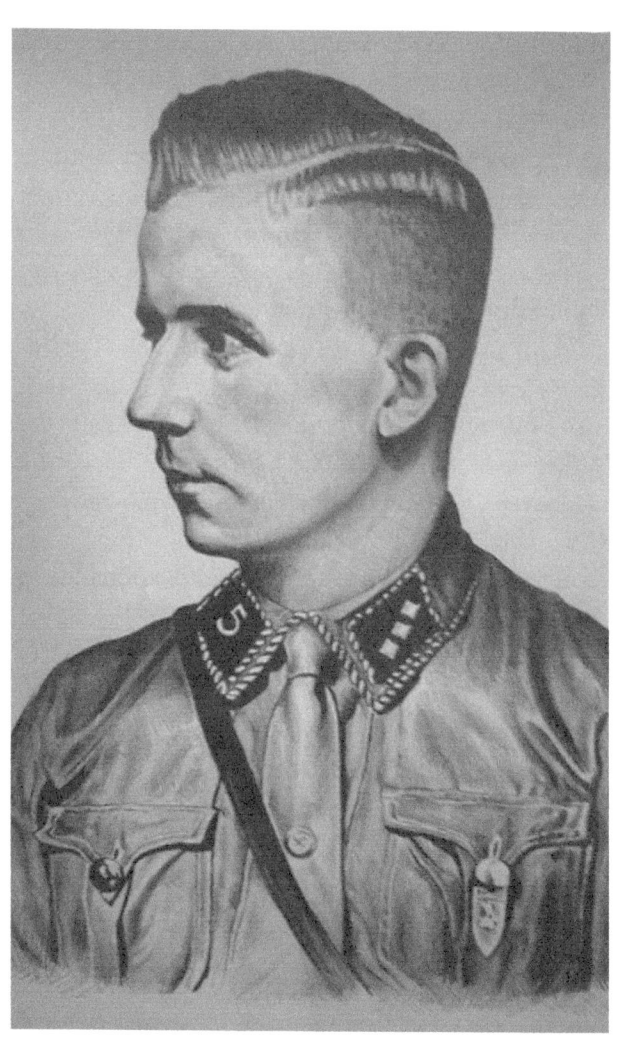

Horst Wessel

Many of the guests, among them Duke Adolf von Mecklenburg, who was standing next to the bride, paid their respects with the Nazi salute.[9]

The pro-German attitude of the Dutch authorities and elites was also confirmed by the German diplomat Wolfgang zu Putlitz, who, in 1938, after four years in London, was assigned to the post of Counsellor in The Hague.

In his autobiography he mentions English politicians who were sympathetic to the Nazi cause, but, as shown by his observations, the situation in the Netherlands was particularly grave: 'In England I had never come across officials in leading agencies who expressed their sympathy for the new Germanism as enthusiastically as in the Netherlands ... The National Socialists of Mr. Mussert (leader of the Dutch Nazis; JHB) had supporters in almost all ministries and even among the royal household ... There were Chiefs of Police who, summarily, at one signal from Butting (attaché at the German embassy, JHB), deported German emigrants at any time of day or night, and handed them over to the Gestapo ... I have never heard that the Dutch government asked for a single document concerning such arbitrary acts, which were known to us by the dozen.'

According to zu Putlitz the Dutch government:

> 'even willingly gave its approval, when, later on, these Dutch involved, who had shown a flagrant disregard for the law, were, at the sugge-

stion of Butting or Schulze-Bernett (specialist in intelligence, JHB), solemnly awarded the order of the German eagle second or third class, which had been created by Hitler'.[10]

Again after the *Kristallnacht* pogrom in November 1938 it became obvious how apprehensive the Dutch authorities were of 'complications abroad'. Now, for the first time in the history of the Netherlands the government decided that the Dutch state would not take care of fugitives. Instead the Dutch Jews themselves had to take pity on several thousand Jewish fugitives from Germany. This was a radical break with the past; during the First World War one million Belgians who fled the war in their own country found shelter in the Netherlands, which was a neutral country. At that time the Dutch government took pity on them. But now, even when the Dutch Jews wanted to help Jewish fugitives from Germany, they were often not permitted to do so.

On the eve of the Second World War, only 7,000 fugitives were allowed to enter the country. Most, among whom were complete families, were considered to be 'undesirable aliens' and were simply sent back to Germany at the frontier, or upon arrival at Schiphol airport from where they were about to leave for England or America.

On 15 November 1938 Dutch prime minister Dr. H. Colijn explained this policy before parliament:

H. Colijn

'... what I will say now comes from the bottom of my heart ... There is another reason why we cannot admit tens and tens of thousands to the Netherlands. I say this in the interest of our Dutch Jews themselves. These days not a single people is free from anti-Semitism; traces of this can also be found in our country and if we were to admit here an unlimited stream of fugitives from abroad, the necessary consequence of this would be that the feeling in our own country with regard to the Jews would swing in an unfavourable way.'[11]

'The government', Colijn added, 'quite seriously has to bear in mind the consequences, all the consequences, including the consequence that were we to say at the moment: we will admit 50,000 people and were it to turn out that the others keep their doors locked, we would be at a loss what to do about those 50,000 people, and this for ever. One should not think that all this is a pleasant position for the government ... , but we also have as our vocation to serve the interests of our own people – not the interests in a lower sense, but also in a higher sense of the word and we hope to be faithful to this'.[12]

Aid from private persons like Gertrude Wijsmuller-Meijer who during the war helped hundreds of Jewish children escape from Germany, was flatly condemned by the Dutch authorities. A press re-

Kristallnacht

lease from the Dutch government exactly a week after the *Kristallnacht* ended with the words:

> 'The behaviour of Dutch people who transfer Jewish children by car or by train to the Netherlands has to be disapproved of. Such a disorderly arrival of fugitives naturally cannot be tolerated. Only an orderly flow is permissible and that to a very limited extent.'[13]

Initial plans to establish a camp for German fugitives in the Elsperterveld in the municipality of Ermelo met with objections from, among others, Queen Wilhelmina, who considered the distance of twelve kilometres that would separate her country residence Het Loo from German asylum-seekers not to be far enough. In 1939, after her intervention, the plan was abandoned and Camp Westerbork was established near the German border, which, by May 1940, sheltered 750 Jewish fugitives from Germany

But Dutch appeasement policy was in vain. On the night of May 9/10th, 1940, German troops invaded the country. Rotterdam was bombed and a five-year occupation followed which saw the murder of approximately three-quarters of Dutch Jews, the execution of numerous hostages, and a vast national trauma.

Among the ruling classes, however, many quickly adapted to the circumstances. Soon after the

Queen Wilhelmina of the Netherlands

German occupation, Dr. Colijn, who had headed four 'crisis governments' and was to become an icon for Dutch political Calvinism, published his book *On the Borderline of Two Worlds*, in which he criticised democracy and recommended acceptance of German domination:

> 'Europe and Germany; Germany and Europe, this will be a relationship to be reckoned with from now until any humanly foreseeable future. One must forget any preference one may have for one thing or another: normally one's influence on the course of things is next to nothing, but in this particular case, it is literally nothing.'[14]

According to the Dutch historian, Louis de Jong, the Netherlands also maintained their tradition of trade during the occupation. He says they possibly preserved this national feature too thoroughly. Dutch trade and industry probably lost touch with the goal of winning the war against the Germans, de Jong argues, because, until the end of 1943, the Dutch fulfilled 84.4 percent of German orders – more even than the French, who achieved 70 percent. According to de Jong, this punctilious discharge of business duties was certainly not absolutely necessary.[15]

In contrast to some Germans, like the Reichskommissar for the Netherlands, Arthur Seyss-Inquart, who was hanged at Nuremberg, most of

D.U.Stikker

the Dutch collaborators escaped punishment after the war. At the end of 1944 Queen Wilhelmina's son-in-law and husband of the future Queen Juliana, Prince Bernhard, thought that purging collaborators in trade and industry was unnecessary. According to the Prince, business would know who had behaved 'unpatriotically' and would clean up its own house.[16] Of 32,232 cases of reported economic collaboration, 61 percent were ignored. The Public Prosecutor only retained an interest in 5,957 cases (18 percent), of which only 500 to 700 were brought before a special court of justice or a tribunal.[17]

Pressure was exerted up to government level to shield suspected industrialists from punishment. From beginning to end, economic and political interests thoroughly influenced the administration of justice. The Foreign Minister, D.U. Stikker, for example, who was a member of the Central Council for purging trade and industry, staved off the imminent punishment of his friend M.H. Damme, director of the Werkspoor company, then Holland's biggest machine factory.[18] It was van Damme who in 1936 had introduced Prince Bernhard into influential trade and commerce circles, and since then he and the Prince had been close friends. Rotterdam's former chief commissioner of police, L. Einthoven, who had collaborated with the Nazis before and during the war, became head of the Bureau of National Security, precursor of the secret service, the *Binnenlandse Veiligheidsdienst*. He also played an important role in purging procedures, which may explain why many collaborators got off scot-free.[19]

Immediately after the war, when the country was liberated, the relationship of the Dutch with the Germans reached an all-time low. Anti-German resentment and orgies of hate against real and alleged collaborators – and their children – were commonplace. But this did not prevent the Dutch economy from intensifying trade relations with Germany at the earliest opportunity.

Nevertheless, many Dutch now regarded themselves as the epitome of virtue and innocence, while every German was considered a villain. The Allies consciously tried to make use of this feeling. The American anthropologist Ruth Benedict was requested by the Office of War Information in Washington to write a memorandum about the Dutch. On the basis of her paper a pamphlet was composed, by which American soldiers could acquire a basic knowledge of the Netherlands to avoid friction with the population.

In her *Note on Dutch Behavior* Benedict points out that 'Dutch self-confidence typically expresses itself, especially among the Calvinist majority, in [the] extreme conviction of having Right on its side'.

With regard to 'American's ignorance of Dutch history and glory' she remarks:

> 'Except in what corresponds to our last years of high school Dutch schools teach practically no history besides that of Holland. Most Dutchmen therefore will be shocked at American ignorance. They should be told that Americans have lived across an ocean in a figurative as well as in a literal sense ... The sense of superiority which Dutch readers will get from this should be a valuable asset, for the Dutch, in contrast to many typical Germans, act with marked consideration and kindness when they feel themselves superior.'[20]

This dialectic of moral superiority, however, was rather flimsy. Anne Frank, for example, was styled as a moral standard bearer of the nation, and in the myth of resistance against the Germans she was illuminated in fairy lights. However, it unfortunately is a fact that this Jewish girl from Frankfurt-am-Main, not only went into hiding in the Dutch capital but was also betrayed by the Dutch.

The facts that most Jewish Dutch, in spite of a sympathy strike in February 1941, received only scant support from the non-Jewish population, and that many Jews were also betrayed by the Dutch, were played down or hushed up.[21] When Simon Wiesenthal explained on Dutch television that the Dutch really could not have done more for the Jews than they actually did (for only few Dutch houses had cellars in which to hide Jews), many people must have heaved a sigh of relief.

Simon Wiesenthal

However, it remains true that tens of thousands of non-Jewish Dutchmen were able to avoid forced labour in Germany by going underground in the Netherlands.

It is also difficult to maintain that the fate of the Jews who were deported was completely unknown to the Dutch population. Even a young girl like Anne Frank, who lived in hiding, had learned from her non-Jewish helper, Miep Gies, about their ultimate fate, and the child believed it. In a diary note of 9 October 1942 she writes:

> 'If even in Holland it is this bad, how will they live in the far and barbarian regions where they are being sent? We assume that most of them will be killed. The English radio speaks of gassing. Maybe that is after all the quickest method of dying.'[22]

After Queen Wilhelmina and the cabinet fled the country, the Dutch civil service actively participated in the preparations for the elimination of Dutch Jews. Several permanent secretaries agreed to the so-called 'declarations of Aryan origin'. It was Dutch policemen who arrested the Jews. And it was Dutch field security officers who guarded them in the Westerbork transit camp, from which they were deported to their death by Dutch railroad personnel.

Many Dutch policemen turned out to be loyal henchmen of the German occupiers. On 24 Sep-

Hanns Albin Rauter

Heinrich Himmler

tember 1942 the Commissioner General of the Security Forces in the Netherlands and Higher Chief of the SS and Police, Hans A. Rauter, informed his superior Heinrich Himmler in a secret letter about the expulsion of the Jews, in the Netherlands:

> 'The new ... Dutch police do an excellent job in the Jewish question and arrest the Jews by the hundreds day and night. In doing so the only risk that occurs is the fact that in places some policemen step out of line and enrich themselves out of Jewish property.'

Himmler's comment at the top of this report was a crisp 'very good'.[23]

The role of the Dutch railways too is a controversial one. In 1944 at the instance of the Allies a railway strike took place in the Netherlands. On 17 September 1945 the first anniversary of this strike was commemorated. During a grand commemoration in The Hague the Minister of Transport and Energy, Ir. T.S.G.J.M. van Schaik, argued in front of the assembled railway personnel:

> 'I understand the struggle you have waged in your hearts when your trains carried off the stolen riches of the Netherlands, when our boys were moved across the border by your trains, or, even worse, to the concentration camps. You did your duty, knowing that in that stage of the war your refusal would have

had consequences even far worse for the Dutch people than what has happened now. Your work served the welfare of the Dutch people but was to the advantage of the enemy at the same time.'[24]

This 'advantage of the enemy' also implied that the Dutch Jews were deported with the help of the Dutch railways. However, according to the government and the railways an earlier strike which might have impeded the deportations was out of the question: 'Going out on strike', thus van Schaik, 'was a matter of balancing advantages and disadvantages, of choosing the lesser of two evils. For the time being the advantage of continuing to run was greater than the disadvantage; the evil attached to the continuation of the company was less than its suspension.'[25]

In other words, during the war the economic interests could not be risked even when the 'lesser evil' implied that the Dutch Jews were sent to their deaths. However, on orders from the Allies this strike was quite possible. All the more so since a strike in September 1944 had only minimal consequences for the Dutch economy: 'The economy of the Netherlands', said van Schaik, 'was *that* (emphasis in original; JHB) paralysed at the time, that your company was hardly necessary for its maintenance.'[26]

Adolf Eichmann

The words of Van Schaik, who did not mention the fate of the Jews at all, were not criticised in the Netherlands but they may shed light on Adolf Eichmann's reported remark that the transports in the Netherlands greased the wheels so perfectly that it was a treat for the eye.

Immediately after the war there was no feeling of guilt among the Dutch authorities or most citizens towards the Dutch Jews. The surviving Jews were not helped by the authorities, but got aid from the American Jewish Joint Distribution Committee. After the war the Dutch government considered the surviving Dutch Jews to be 'Dutchmen like all Dutchmen'. For the authorities Jewishness had no special meaning. This insensitivity led to excesses. In two prisoner camps in Valkenburg and Sittard 170 German Jews were detained amidst captured SS members and collaborators. Before the war these German Jews had been granted asylum in the Netherlands. During the war they were deported to Bergen-Belsen and after their liberation they returned to the Netherlands where they were detained as 'Germans'.[27]

In the first twenty years after the war most Dutch people gave hardly any thought to the fate of Jewish fellow-countrymen. The attention was entirely fixed on the resistance against the Germans and the occupation in general. This was the time when the myth of the Netherlands as a 'country of resistance' developed; a myth that was willingly received abroad. There was more attention paid to the non-Jewish Dutch resistance fighters who had been detained in the concentration camps than for the Jews who had been killed there. In this respect there was little difference with the situation in the German Democratic Republic.[28]

Many examples can be cited of the callous attitude which Jewish survivors encountered in the Netherlands until well into the Sixties. To take one example: During the war Jewish Dutch were forced to surrender their money, stock-holdings, jewellery and works of art to the bank Lippmann Rosenthal & Co for which they received a receipt. The Jewish possessions, however, were bartered away by the bank against rated values that were much too low. After the war some of these goods could not be claimed by their owners or their descendants. In 1968-69 civil servants from the Amsterdam branch office of the Ministry of Finance decided to sell among themselves for a symbolic amount what was left of the booty - valuables like earrings, watches, gold fountain pens and silver cutlery. There was so much interest among the officials of the Ministry that they decided to draw lots.[29] Nobody had the idea of informing the Jewish community.

There are suspicions that many valuables that were stolen from the Dutch Jews remained in the Netherlands. This amounts to tens of thousands of houses, estates, artworks and stocks and shares belonging to war victims like gypsies, homosexuals and Jehovah's Witnesses as well as Jews. Often these possessions fell into the hands of Dutch collaborators.

The restitution of art collections too, did not always work out according to the regulations. After the war paintings that were stolen for the most part from the Netherlands, were stored by the Council of Dutch Art Collection (SNK) which was responsible for tracing the owners or their descendants and returning their property. However, this was only done in a few hundred cases. Today this collection still contains 3,500 paintings. From the correspondence of the *SNK* it appears that this organisation, immediately after the war, tried to change the laws involved in such a way, that the works of art 'naturally can be taken over by the state ... in cases eligible for that purpose'.[30]

An example of this dubious policy is the case of Jewish art-dealer Jacques Goudstikker, who, in 1940, in the course of his flight from Amsterdam to England, was killed in an accident. During the occupation Goudstikker's paintings were to a large extent 'purchased' by Göring at bargain prices. After the war the Dutch state recovered 300 works of art from the Goudstikker collection, half of which were sold and the other half presented to Dutch museums. The heirs did not get anything.

Under pressure from the Dutch authorities Goudstikker's widow agreed in 1952 that her tax arrears should be cancelled in return for her giving up her husband's possessions. When, in 1997, this case became known in the United States, it gave rise to bad publicity for the Dutch. Subsequently the Dutch Ministry of Education and Cultural Affairs engaged the PR-agency *Hill & Knowlton* to make sure that the issue of looted art in the Netherlands would in future, according to a spokesman of the ministry, 'be presented in the American media in an appropriate way'. However, it is almost certain that *Hill & Knowlton*, which maintains good relations with TV-stations, local and national newspapers, industrialists and politicians, managed to prevent CNN from broadcasting a report on the Goudstikker case.[31]

Until recently Dutch historians were expected not to question the myth that the Netherlands were a 'country of resistance' against the Germans. When, in an interview in 1993, Dutch historian Graa Boomsma compared the employment of military forces in the Dutch colony Indonesia after the Second World War with the conduct of the *SS*, this was enough to have him persecuted for slander. Ironic indeed, considering the fact that there is circumstantial evidence that many Dutch who served in the German *SS* were sent after the war for their 'rehabilitation' to Indonesia to maintain colonial order.[32]

After the judges had cleared Boomsma, the public prosecutor's office filed an appeal, which was quite unusual. In May 1994 the international association of writers, *PEN*, expressed its anxiety about the planned action against Boomsma in a letter to the Dutch Justice Minister Hirsch Ballin.[33] At the beginning of 1995 the suit was again dismissed, but this official action was a clear signal to Dutch historians to tread carefully when assessing the colonial past and the role of the Dutch in the Second World War.

Such taboos belong to the past. The myth of the Dutch who resisted the Germans on a massive scale and suffered because of the fate of their Jewish compatriots, is being rapidly refuted by the overwhelming evidence. However, much of this evidence is not new and it looks as if the current, more differentiated view of the Netherlands and their relationship with Nazi Germany also serves contemporary Dutch-German interests.

The current Dutch government is anxious not to disturb relationships with its neighbouring country, not least because of the economic dependency of the Netherlands upon unified Germany. Attempts are therefore being made to improve the image of Germany in the Netherlands and to establish a cordial relationship. These efforts, which are strongly supported by the royal family, are very vigorously pursued. At the beginning of 1995, Dutch newspapers reported that the government of Social Democratic prime minister Wim Kok was trying to raise half a million guilders to finance a publicity campaign aimed at the development of a 'feeling' expressing 'togetherness-with-the-Germans'.[34] Many Dutch historians, journalists and politicians nowadays support this political line by drawing attention to Dutch complicity in Nazi crimes, while focusing at the same time on Germany's post-war democracy. Whether this will breed solidarity between neighbours in 'Unified Europe' is doubtful.[35] The Dutch Jews, moreover, may find that such a 'feeling' adds insult to injury.

Literature

R.F. Benedict, *A Note on Dutch behavior*. A complete edition of this text in: R. van Ginkel, Notities over Nederlanders, Antropologische Reflecties (Notes about Dutchmen. Anthropological reflections). Amsterdam/Meppel, 1997, 225 - 234. here: 226 and 232.

J.H. Brinks, About Mammon and Morals. Some Remarks on the Ambivalent Relationship of the Dutch with the Germans, *The Mediterranean Quarterly*, vol. 8, nr 4, Fall 1997, 123-130.

H.Colijn, Saevis Tranquillus in Undis. Toelichting op het Antirevolutionair Beginselprogram, Tweede druk, waarin opgenomen 'Op de grens van Twee Werelden', Amsterdam, 1940, 581-615; here 609. (Saevis Tranquillus in Undis. Elucidation of the Anti-Revolutionary Manifesto, second edition, which contains >On the Borderline of Two Worlds<, Amsterdam, 1940).

L. de Jong, *Het Koninkrijk der Nederlanden in de Tweede Wereldoorlog*, (The Kingdom of the Netherlands in the Second World War), part 2, The Hague: Martinus Nijhoff, 1969, 153; and part 7, (May '43 - June '44, first half) 1976, 120-30: here especially 130.

J.P. Meihuizen, *Farce. De Bestraffing van Economische Collaboratie 1944-1951* (Farce. The Punishment of Economic Collaboration 1944-1951), Amsterdam, 1998.

J. Presser, *The Destruction of the Dutch Jews*, New York, Dutton, 1969.

F. van Vree, *De Nederlandse Pers en Duitsland 1930-1939. Een Studie over de Vorming van de Publieke Opinie* (The Dutch Press and Germany 1930-1939. A Study of the Formation of Public Opinion) Historische Uitgeverij Groningen, 1989.

N. van der Zee, *Om erger te voorkomen. De Voorbereiding en Uitvoering van de Vernietiging van het Nederlandse Jodendom tijdens de Tweede Wereldoorlog* (To prevent worse. The Preparation and Execution of the Destruction of Dutch Jewry during the Second World War), Amsterdam, 1997.

Abridged version of this article in: *History Today*, Vol. 49 (6), June 1999, 17-23.

Notes:

1 Cp. N. van der Zee, Om erger te voorkomen. De voorbereiding en uitvoering van de vernietiging van het Nederlandse jodendom tijdens de Tweede Wereldoorlog.

(To prevent worse. The preparation and execution of the destruction of Dutch Jewry during the Second World War), Amsterdam, 1997, 40.

2   Withdrawal of Missions and Consuls. Subenclosure. Report of the Netherlands Minister relating to conditions in Petrograd, in: *Publications of the Department of State, Papers relating to the Foreign Relations of the United States. 1918. Russia.* (In three Volumes); here Vol. 1, United States Government Printing Office, Washington, D.C., 1931, 675-679; here. 678 and 679.

3   In 1997 Dutch historian Ger van Roon stumbled in a new *Bundesarchiv* in Berlin upon files with official notices about trips of Dutch officials to the *Gestapo* at the Prinz Albrechtstrasse and the *Kriminalpolizei* at the Alexanderplatz. Cp: H. Goudriaan, Politietop al vroeg contact met Gestapo (Police top already early in contact with Gestapo), *Trouw*, 18 december, 1997; also: H. Goudriaan, Latere BVD-chef Einthoven op namenlijst Gestapo (Future chief of BVD [National Security Service] Einthoven on list of names of Gestapo), *Trouw*, 18 December, 1997.

4   Quoted in: H. Goudriaan, Politietop al vroeg contact met Gestapo (Police top already early in contact with Gestapo), *Trouw*, 18 december, 1997. The advice to shelter fugitives in concen-

tration camps was less surprising than it may seem at first sight. In those days the Netherlands themselves kept two concentration camps in New Guinea. Indonesian dissidents, among whom was the later prime minister Hatta, were kept there for years often without trial. Many of them died prematurely as a result of hardships.

5   Ibidem.

6   H. Goudriaan, Latere BVD-chef Einthoven op namenlijst Gestapo (Future chief of BVD [National Security Service] Einthoven on list of names of Gestapo), *Trouw*, 18-12-1997.

7   Pieter Geyl explains that van Blankenstein was sacked because 'a Jew as foreign correspondent, that was considered dangerous in Rotterdam'. See Pieter Geyl, *Pennestrijd*, Groningen: Wolters, 1971, 340.

8   In 1935, the Germans had announced an advertisement boycott. The German envoy in The Hague, the consul in Rotterdam, and the press officer of the Foreign Ministry informed the director of the newspaper that it had been especially the articles of van Blankenstein that caused this measure. Frank van Vree, *De Nederlandse Pers en Duitsland 1930-1939. Een studie over de vorming van de publieke opinie* (The Dutch press and Germany 1930-1939.

A study of the formation of public opinion) Historische Uitgeverij Groningen: 1989, 131. The renowned Dutch journalist Menno ter Braak, too, became a victim of the *zeitgeist*. On the eve of the Second World War, he was caught up in a remarkable accusation. Because of his critical comments about Hitler in a preface to Hermann Rauschning's *Hitler speaks*, he was charged with 'slander of a friendly head of state', as Lord Chancellor Pieter Sjoerd Gerbrandy said on the first of May 1940. Cp. Louis De Jong, *Het Koninkrijk der Nederlanden in de Tweede Wereldoorlog*, (The Kingdom of the Netherlands in the Second World War), part 2, The Hague: Martinus Nijhoff, 1969, 153.

9 J. Kroon, Vijftig jaar huwelijksleven in een glazen huis (Fifty years of marriage in a glass house), *NRC Handelsblad*, 3 January, 1987; also: G-J, Laan, R. Robijns, Het geheim van Soestdijk. Prins Bernhard gaat in zaken (The secret of Soestdijk. Prince Bernhard goes into business), *Het Vrije Volk*, 17 December, 1977.

10 W. zu Putlitz, *In Rok tussen de Bruinhemden. Herinneringen van een Duits diplomaat* (In Evening Dress among the Brownshirts. Memories of a German Diplomat), The Hague, 1964, 210.

11 Redevoering van Minister President Dr. Colijn op 15 november 1938 in de Tweede Kamer, 13e vergadering, 15 November 1938, Algemeene beraadslagingen over de Rijksbegroting voor het dienstjaar 1939, *Handelingen der Staten-Generaal 1938-1939 - Tweede Kamer*, 262. (Address of prime minister Dr. Colijn on 15. November 1938 in the Lower House, 13th meeting, 15 November 1938, General deliberations about the national budget for the official year 1939, Proceedings of the Dutch Lower House of the States-General 1938-1939, 262.)

12 Ibidem, 269.

13 Quoted in: N. van der Zee, *Om erger te voorkomen* (To prevent worse), 37.

14 H. Colijn, Saevis Tranquillus in Undis. Toelichting op het antirevolutionair Beginselprogram, Tweede druk, waarin opgenomen 'Op de grens van Twee Werelden', Amsterdam, 1940, 581-615; here 609. (Elucidation of the anti-revolutionary manifesto, which contains >On the borderline of Two Worlds<).

15 L. de Jong, *Het Koninkrijk der Nederlanden in de Tweede Wereldoorlog*, (The Kingdom of the Netherlands in the Second World War), part 7, (May '43 - June '44, first half), The Hague, 1976, 120-30: here especially 130.

16 J.P. Meihuizen, *Farce. De bestraffing van economische collaboratie 1944-1951* (Farce. The punishment of economic collaboration 1944-1951), Amsterdam, 1998, 5, 6.

17 Ibidem, 38, 39.

18 Ibidem, 21, 22.

19 R. van den Brink, Hitlers Orders. Nederlandse ambtenaren waren al fout vóór de oorlog (Hitlers Orders. Dutch officials acted already wrongly before the war), *Vrij Nederland*, 10 January, 1998, 14-16; 14.

20 R. F. Benedict, *A Note on Dutch behavior*. A complete edition of this text in: R. van Ginkel, Notities over Nederlanders, Antropologische Reflecties (Notes about Dutchmen. Anthropological reflections). Amsterdam/Meppel, 1997, 225 – 234; here: 226 and 232.

21 Probably one of the best presentations of the persecution of the Jewish Dutch in Holland during the Second World War can be found in Jacob Presser, *The Destruction of the Dutch Jews*, New York, Dutton, 1969.

22 A. Frank, *Het Achterhuis. Dagboekbrieven 12 juni 1942-augustus 1944*, Amsterdam, Contact, 1947, 39; quoted in: N. van der Zee, *Om erger te voorkomen* (To avoid worse), 127.

23 Facsimile reproduction of this letter in: J. Presser *Ondergang. De vervolging en verdelging van het Nederlandse Jodendom (1940-1945)* (Destruction. The persecution and extermination of Dutch Jewry 1940-1945), Part I, The Hague, 1985, 280 ff.

24 Rede van de minister van Verkeer en Energie, Ir. T.S.G.J.M. van Schaik tijdens de herdenkingsbijeenkomst van de spoorwegstaking op 17 September 1944 in het gebouw van de groenten- en vruchtenveiling in Den Haag op 17 September 1945. *Plechtige Herdenking van de Spoorwegstaking op 17 September 1945, Rotterdam*, 1946, 21-27; here: 24. (Address of minister of Transport and Energy, Ir. T.S.G.J.M. van Schaik during the commemoration of the railway strike on 17 September 1944 in the building of the vegetable and fruit auction hall in The Hague on 17 September 1945. Solemn commemoration of the railway strike on 17 September 1945, Rotterdam, 1946, 21-27; here: 24.)

25 Ibidem.

26 Ibidem, 25.

27 F. Peeters, Eenzaam, Berooid, ontheemd – en toch als iedereen (Lonely, destitute, homeless – and yet like everybody else). *Het Parool*, PS, 13 December 1997; cp.: B. Haveman, Thuis na de

Holocaust (At home after the Holocaust), *De Volkskrant*, Vervolg, 20 December, 1997.

28 Cp. J.H. Brinks, Political Anti-Fascism in the German Democratic Republic, *Journal of Contemporary History*, vol. 32, nr 2, April 1997, 207-217.

29 J. Houwink ten Cate, Niet historici, maar politici moeten Liro-zaak afwikkelen (Not historians but politicians must settle Liro-affair), *De Volkskrant*, 20 December, 1997, also: Joods eigendom onderhands geveild (Jewish property auctioned privately), *NRC-Handelsblad*, 10 December, 1997; Nazi-buit bij ambtenaren (Nazi booty with civil servants), *Algemeen Dagblad*, 10 December 1997.

30 P. den Hollander, Staat aasde op roofkunst (State had its eye on stolen art), *Algemeen Dagblad*, 12 December, 1997; also: L. Heyting, De kous is nog niet af. Verdwenen kunst, verdwenen eigenaren en talloze claims van regeringen en particulieren (There's still no end to the matter. Disappeared art, disappeared owners and countless claims of governments and private persons), *NRC Handelsblad*, Cultureel supplement, 28 November, 1997.

31 S. Weidemann, ‚Ein schäbiger Vergleich'. Klage zurückgewiesen: Die Niederlande tricksen Beutekunst-Erben aus (A shabby exchange. Case

dismissed: The Netherlands outwit the heirs to looted art), *Süddeutsche Zeitung*, 16 March, 1999.

32 Martin van Amerongen, Contrapunt. Reclassering anno 1949 (Counterpoint. Rehabilitation in the year 1949), *De Groene Amsterdammer*, 15 September, 1993. See also C. van Esterik, Het litteken van een scheermes: SS'ers in Nederlands-Indië tijdens de politiële acties (The scar of a razor: Members of the SS during police actions in the Netherlands East Indies), *NRC-Handelsblad*, 24 November 1984. In 1997, many former Dutch members of the SS put in an application for a pension from Germany, when it was made public that Germany has paid war pensions to former members of the SS and war criminals all over the world. See, for example, Keine Opferrente mehr für Adolf Hitler (No victim pension for Adolf Hitler anymore), *Süddeutsche Zeitung*, 28 February, 1997.

33 Brief aan minister Hirsch Ballin: PEN protesteert tegen vervolging auteur Boomsma. (Letter to minister Hirsch Ballin: PEN protests against proceedings against author Boomsma) *NRC- Handelsblad*, 24 May 1994; also: *Index on Censorship*, London: Writers and Scholars International, 3/94: 179, 4-5/94: 245, 2/95: 181.

34 E. Nysingh, Half miljoen gezocht voor 'wij-gevoel' Duitsland en Nederland (Wanted: Half a million guilders for Dutch 'Feeling' Expressing 'togetherness-with-the-Germans'). *De Volkskrant*, 26 January, 1995.

35 An official investigation into this matter of November 1997 shows that in spite of, but probably because of all official efforts to improve the image of Germany in the Netherlands, Dutch youngsters, just like in 1993 and 1995, considered Germany to be the least sympathetic country of all member states of the European Union. In: H. Dekker, R. Aspeslagh, B. Winkel, *Burenverdriet. Attituden ten aanzien van de lidstaten van de Europese Unie* (Neighbourly sorrows. Attitudes towards member states of the European Union), Netherlands institute of international relations Clingendael, The Hague, 1997. The Dutch Ministry of Foreign Affairs that subsidises this (serial) investigation subsequently explained that *Clingendael* may continue its research, but is not allowed to publish the results any more. A. Vaessen, Duitsers boos over studies (Germans angry at studies), *Algemeen Dagblad*, 5 March 1998. According to Dutch Minister for Foreign Affairs, Hans van Mierlo, history teaching is to blame for Germany's negative image as it 'ends with the year 1945'. (S. Weidemann, Verhältnis so gut wie nie zuvor

(Relationship as well as never before), *Süddeutsche Zeitung*, 21/22 March, 1998.